'If we want to know what it means to be mortal, we need look no further than the Man in Black'

BOB DYLAN

'His influence spread over many generations. I loved him as a singer and writer'

MICK JAGGER

'I lost my innocence with Johnny Cash'

NICK CAVE

'He's always there, the tallest figure in the circle of integrity, the deepest voice when night comes down, and the bravest take on sanity in the midst of wild confusion'

LEONARD COHEN

'Johnny Cash has always been larger than life'

KRIS KRISTOFFERSON

FOREVER
WORDS

JOHNNY CASH
FOREVER WORDS

THE UNKNOWN POEMS

edited and introduced by PAUL MULDOON
foreword by JOHN CARTER CASH

CANONGATE

Published in Great Britain in 2016 by Canongate Books Ltd, 14 High Street,
Edinburgh EH1 1TE

www.canongate.co.uk

1

This edition first published in the United States in 2016 by
Blue Rider Press, an imprint of Penguin Random House LLC
375 Hudson Street, New York, New York 10014

Blue Rider Press is a registered trademark and its colophon is a trademark of
Penguin Random House LLC

British Library Cataloguing-in-Publication Data
A catalogue record for this book is available on
request from the British Library

ISBN 978 1 78211 994 4

Book design by Lauren Kolm

Printed and bound in Great Britain by Clays Ltd, St Ives plc.

CONTENTS

FOREWORD: REDEMPTIONS

My father had many faces. There was much that made up the man. If you think you "know" John R Cash, think again. There are many layers, so much beneath the surface.

First, I knew him to be fun. Within the first six years of my life, if asked what Dad was to me I would have emphatically responded: "Dad is fun!" This was my simple foundation for my enduring relationship with my father.

This is the man he was. He never lost this.

To those who knew him well—family, friends, coworkers alike—the one essential thing that was blazingly evident was the light and laughter within my father's heart. Typically, though his common image may be otherwise, he was not heavy and dark, but loving and full of color.

Yet there was so much more . . .

For one thing—he was brilliant. He was a scholar, learned in ancient texts, including those of Flavius Josephus and unquestionably of the Bible. He was an ordained minister and could easily hold his own with any theologian. His books on ancient history, such as Gibbon's *The History of the Decline and Fall of the Roman Empire*, were annotated, read, reread, and worn, his very soul deeply ingrained into their threadbare pages. I still have some of these books. When I hold them, when I touch the pages, I can sense my father in some ways even more profoundly than in his music.

My father was an entertainer. This is, of course, one of the most marked and enduring manifestations. There are thousands upon thousands of new Johnny Cash fans every year, inspired by the music, talent, and—I believe hugely—by the mystery of the man.

My dad was a poet. He saw the world through unique glasses, with simplicity, spirituality, and humor. He loved a good story and was quick to find comedy, even in bleak circumstances. This is evident in one of the last songs he wrote within his lifetime, "Like the 309":

> It should be a while before I see Dr. Death
> So it would sure be nice if I could get my breath

Well, I'm not the crying nor the whining kind
Till I hear the whistle of the 309
Of the 309, of the 309
Put me in my box on the 309.

Take me to the depot, put me to bed
Blow an electric fan on my gnarly old head
Everybody take a look, see I'm doing fine
Then load my box on the 309
On the 309, on the 309
Put me in my box on the 309.

Dad was asthmatic and had great difficulty breathing during the last months of his life. On top of all this, he suffered with recurring bouts of pneumonia. Still, through the gift of laughter, he found the strength to face these infirmities. This recording is steeped in irony, although made mere days before his passing. His voice is weak, yet the mirth in his soul rings true.

Dad was many things, yes. He was tortured throughout his life by sadness and addiction. His tragic youth was marked by the loss of his best friend and brother Jack, who died as the result of a horrible accident when John R was only twelve. Jack was a deeply spiritual young man, kind and protective of his two-years-younger brother. Perhaps it was this sadness and mourning that partly defined my father's poetry and songs throughout his life. He was likewise defined at the end of his life by the loss of my mother, June Carter. When she passed, their love was more beautiful than ever before: unconditional and kind.

Still, it could not be said that any of this—darkness, love, sadness, music, joy, addiction—wholly defined the man. He was all of these things and none of them. Complicated, but what could be said that speaks the essential truth? What prevails? The music, of course . . . but also . . . *the words.*

All that made up my father is to be found in this book, within these "forever words."

When my parents died, they left behind a monstrous amassment of "stuff." They just didn't throw anything away. Each and every thing was a treasure, but none more than my father's handwritten letters, poems, and documents, ranging through the entirety of his life. There was a huge amount of paper—his studies of the book of Job, his handwritten autobiography *Man in Black*, his letters to my mother, and those to his first wife, Vivian, from the 1950s. Dad was a writer, and he never ceased. His writings ranged through every stage of his life: from the poems of a naive yet undeniably brilliant sixteen-year-old to later comprehensive studies on the life of the Apostle Paul. The more I have looked, the more I have understood of the man.

When I hold these papers, I feel his presence within the handwriting; it brings him back to me. I remember how he held his pen, how his hand shook a bit, but how careful and proud he was of his penmanship—and how determined and courageous he was. Some of these pages are stained with coffee, perhaps the ink smudged.

When I read these pages, I feel the love he carried in those hands. I once again feel the closeness of my father, how he cared so deeply for the creative endeavor; how he cared for his loved ones.

There are some of these I feel he would have wanted to be shared, some whose genius and brilliance simply demanded to be heard. I hope and believe the ones chosen within this book are those he would want read by the world.

Finally, it is not only the strength of his poetic voice that speaks to me, it is his very life enduring and coming anew with these writings. It is in these words my father sings a new song, in ways he has never done before. Now, all these years past, the *words* tell a full tale; with their release, he is with us again, speaking to our hearts, making us laugh, and making us cry.

The music will endure, this is true. But also, the *words*. It is ultimately evident within these words that the sins and sadnesses have failed, that goodness commands and triumphs. To me, this book is a redemption, a cherished healing. *Forever.*

John Carter Cash
35,000 feet above western Arkansas, flying east . . .

INTRODUCTION

I.

The great artist has a finger on the pulse of his time; he also quickens that pulse. In the case of Johnny Cash, his music seems to well up directly from the poverty and deprivation of country life in the Great Depression, through the uncertainty of World War II, the Cold War, Korea, and Vietnam, to the victories of adulation and the vicissitudes of addiction. We might guess, even if we didn't know, that Cash's classic "Five Feet High and Rising" is an account of the flooding with which he was all too familiar from his 1930s childhood in the cotton fields of Arkansas:

How high's the water, mama?
Five feet high and risin'
How high's the water, papa?
Five feet high and risin'

His song "Man in Black" is a deft and dexterous comment on Vietnam, a subject on which so many others were heavy-handed:

And I wear it for the thousands who have died,
Believin' that the Lord was on their side
I wear it for another hundred thousand who have died,
Believin' that we all were on their side

The relationship between the amphitheater and amphetamines, meanwhile, is rather neatly delineated in a piece collected here called "Going, Going, Gone":

Liquid, tablet, capsule, powder
Fumes and smoke and vapor
The payoff is the same in the end
Liquid, tablet, capsule, powder
Fumes and smoke and vapor
Convenient ways to get the poison in

So ingrained in our collective unconscious is the voice of Johnny Cash that we can all but hear the *boom-chicka boom-chicka* of his guitar accompaniment, at once reassuring and disquieting in its very familiarity.

The defining characteristic of an effective lyric—even the greatest of them—is that it doesn't quite hold up to the scrutiny we might bring to bear on a poem, that only something along the lines of that missing *boom-chicka* will allow it to be completely what it most may be. In the case of work that is previously unpublished, or hitherto overlooked, this intrinsic lack is thrown into even greater relief. Is it possible that Cash himself chose not to round out, never mind record, some or all of these pieces? Are we doing him and his memory a disservice in allowing them out of the attic and into the wider world? Writers of the stature of Elizabeth Bishop, T. S. Eliot, and Philip Larkin are among those whose reputations have suffered at least a dent from the indiscriminate publication of their second- or third-rate efforts. And the fact is that even great artists not only nod, like Homer, but also produce nonstarters and no-nos.

Such considerations weighed heavily on the team—John Carter Cash and Steve Berkowitz—most immediately involved in the collection and collation of the copious raw material from which I was able to make this selection. It was with an initial sense of relief, then an increasingly rapturous glee, that I realized there is so much here that will indeed broaden and deepen our perception of Johnny Cash and his legacy.

II.

Before thinking about Johnny Cash's legacy, though, I'd like to appeal to a passage from T. S. Eliot's "Tradition and the Individual Talent," which I continue to find particularly instructive in this matter:

No poet, no artist of any art, has his complete meaning alone. His significance, his appreciation is the appreciation of his relation to the dead poets and artists. You cannot value him alone; you must set him, for contrast and comparison, among the dead. I mean this as a principle of aesthetic, not merely historical, criticism. The necessity that he shall conform, that he shall cohere, is not one-sided; what happens when a new work of art is created is something that happens simultaneously to all the works of art which preceded it.

The veracity of Eliot's last profound observation may be seen in a piece like "The Dogs Are in the Woods":

The dogs are in the woods
And the huntin's lookin' good
And the raccoons on the hill
I can hear them trailing still

These dogs are calling out to some of their not-too-distant relatives, the hunting hounds poisoned by Lord Randall's dissed girlfriend, as reported by Lord Randall to his mother in the traditional Scotch-Irish folksong "Lord Randall":

> "What became of your bloodhounds, Lord Randall my son?
> What became of your bloodhounds, my handsome young man?"
> "O they swelled and they died: mother, make my bed soon,
>   for I'm weary wi' hunting, and fain wald lie down."

We've already seen the dialogue format of the "Lord Randall" ballad repurposed in "Five Feet High and Rising." The "Muscadine Wine" we find in this collection is an offshoot of the same vine that gave us the blood-red wine in the Scottish standard "The Ballad of Sir Patrick Spens":

> The King sits in Dunfermline town,
>   Drinking the blood-red wine;
> "O where shall I get a skeely skipper
>   To sail this ship or mine?"
>
> Then up and spake an eldern knight,
>   Sat at the King's right knee:
> "Sir Patrick Spens is the best sailor
>   That ever sailed the sea."

The King has written a broad letter,
And sealed it with his hand,
And sent it to Sir Patrick Spens,
Was walking on the strand.

It's no accident that the tradition of the Scots ballad, along with its transmogrified versions in North America, is one in which Johnny Cash should be so at ease, given that the first recorded instance of the name Cash—that of Roger Cass—is found in, of all things, the *Registrum de Dunfermelyn*. The entry is dated 1130, during the reign of King David I of Scotland (r. 1124–1153). "The Ballad of Sir Patrick Spens" is set in Dunfermline a mere hundred sixty years later, in 1290.

We may also see the influence of the Scotch-Irish tradition in the use of the tag phrase at the end of each verse (a device we've come to associate with the work of Bob Dylan), in a piece like "Slumgullion":

Every day's a brand-new mountain
Don't drink long at any fountain
You'll be turned into slumgullion

"Slumgullion" is a word that means several things, including a watery stew, the watery waste left after the rendering of whale blubber, and the slurry associated with a mine. It is generally believed to be derived from "slum," an old word for "slime," and "gullion," an English dialect term for "mud" or "cesspool." "Gullion" may actually be a corruption of the Gaelic word *góilín*, "pit" or "pool." The earliest recorded usage of "slumgullion," in Mark Twain's *Roughing It* (1872), refers to a drink:

> Then he poured for us a beverage which he called "Slum gullion," and it is hard to think he was not inspired when he named it. It really pretended to be tea, but there was too much dish-rag, and sand, and old bacon-rind in it to deceive the intelligent traveler.

The Scotch-Irish song tradition has a strong humorous component that may be detected in "Jellico Coal Man," a song about life in a Tennessee mining town that could easily have been called Slumgullion had it not already been named after the wild angelica (*Angelica sylvestris*) that grows there in abundance:

> It will warm your baby in the winter time
> It comes direct from the Jellico mine
> When the sun comes up that's the time I start
> You will see me comin' with my two-wheel cart

There's a not too-far-from-the-surface eroticism about this coal-mining man that straddles not only the ballad tradition but also the bawdiness of certain old blues songs. We recognize it in "Hey, Baby, Wake Up," with its assertion that "I need my biscuit buttered, Babe." We have detected it in "Who's Gonna Grease My Skillet?" when he says "Who's gonna squeeze my juice if you should go," with a nod and wink in the direction of Robert Johnson's "Squeeze my lemon."

In addition to conjuring up the naughty nickname attached to, say, Jelly Roll Morton, "Jellico Coal Man" brings to mind the city of Jericho, the walls of which succumbed to the power of music when the Israelite priests sounded their ram's-horn trumpets. (In one of those fascinating coincidences that many of us enjoy, Jellico was the childhood home of Homer Rodeheaver, the famous evangelist and trombonist.) The iconography of the Bible is a constant in Johnny Cash's work, rarely so powerful as in a piece like "Job," with its recalibration of Job as cattle baron:

> Job was a wealthy man
> He had a lot of kids and a lot of land
> He had cattle on a thousand hills
> He lived every day to do God's will

On a technical note, there exist a number of versions of the "Job" text in Cash's hand. As with several other pieces included here, I drew on these multiple manuscript sources to make a plausible "finished" version. An attentive reader may therefore remark on discrepancies and disconnects, variations and vagaries, between the printed texts and the facsimile material with which they're so artfully interspersed. That reader may also notice the rationalization of stanza breaks and the generally normative tendencies of grammar, punctuation, and spelling. Cash's occasional misspellings need be perpetuated no more than Yeats's, and that includes the humorous humdinger "Caddilac."

There's another humorous strand running through a number of these lyrics that draws on the cowboy tradition, be it the Lone Ranger mounted on Silver, referred to in "Spirit Rider" ("I will mount my Hi-Yo and I will ride off, ma'am"), or the singing cowboy Roy Rogers in "Hey, Baby, Wake Up":

> Hey, Baby, wake up
> Did you hear the latest news
> The man said Roy and Dale split up
> And Dale got Trigger, too
> Yeah, I hear your sweet feet on the floor
> I knew that'd get through to you

That humor extends to the litany of exhortations in "Don't Make a Movie About Me" that reflect Cash's own ambivalence about celebrity and the associated tabloid slobbering:

Don't let 'em drag old Hickory Lake
For my telephones and bottles and roller skates . . .
Out a hundred yards from my lakeside house
Weighted down with a rock is a skirt and blouse
A dozen pair of boots that made a dozen corns
Trombones, trumpets, harmonicas and horns
And the tapes that I threw from the lakeside door
Silverstein, and Kristofferson from years before

This was the selfsame Shel Silverstein who won the Grammy
Award for Best Country Song of 1969 for "A Boy Named Sue." He
was friendly with David Allan Coe, also mentioned in "Don't Make
a Movie About Me," who had the distinction of embarking on his
music career in Nashville while living in a hearse parked outside
Ryman Auditorium, a macabre touch that would surely have ap-
pealed to Cash. The song continues:

If they're hot on a book called *Man in Black*
Tell 'em I've got the rights and won't give back
If you don't know my tune you can't get it right
I don't talk about me in *Man in White*

As it turns out, *Man in White* is the title of Cash's historical novel
about the life of Saint Paul before and after his conversion. We're

reminded, of course, that Johnny Cash as the "Man in Black" is less gunslinger than psalm-singing preacher, the unapologetic nature of his Christian faith shining through in "He Bore It All for Me," a piece that takes as its text Matthew 11:28, "Come unto me, all ye that labour and are heavy laden, and I will give you rest." A faith in the sense that there is a world beyond this one must at least partly inform the sentiments of "Forever":

> But the trees that I planted
> Still are young
> The songs I sang
> Will still be sung

III.

In addition to the sense that it functions within time, the great work of art brings with it a profound sense of timelessness. There's a sense of immortality and inevitability that suggests (1) that it has always existed and (2) that it was always meant to exist in this form and this form only. Johnny Cash's quiet insistence that his songs "will still be sung" might easily be read as self-regarding but is more accurately perceived as a manifestation of the humility that is an absolute pre-requisite in art-making: it has less to do with his name and fame being bruited about in Dubai or Decatur or Dunfermline itself than with his achieving a kind of beautiful anonymity. It's a claim to deathlessness that may be made only by someone who has taken into account that, like "The Ballad of Sir Patrick Spens," Johnny Cash's brilliant "California Poem" was written by everyone and no one:

> The lights are on past midnite
> The curtains closed all day
> There's trouble on the mountain
> The valley people say

> *Paul Muldoon*

FOREVER WORDS

BALLAD OF JOHNNY CAPMAN

1970s

Johnny Capman said
To his wife one day
I'm sorry, my dear
But I just can't stay
My country calls
And I'm on my way

His wife said to him
You must stay
We are in trouble
And you can't go away

The war has come
And the growing is hard
The soil is tough
As our front yard

If you leave me
What can we eat

We have no clothes
Or shoes on our feet

Johnny Capman said
To his wife again
There's a war to fight
I will join the men

The days went by
Not a word was said
For fear that he
Would come back dead

About a week from then
A letter came
She tried to find
Her Johnny's name

But it was not from him
And the letter said
We regret to tell you
Your Johnny's dead

BIG-HEARTED GIRL

Undated

You've done every dirty thing
That a woman shouldn't do
You're polished in the ways of the world
But when you run your velvet fingers
Through the troubles in my head
I'm glad you're a big-hearted girl

Big-hearted girl, spread yourself around
But remember me when you get back to town

You've broken every rule
That a lover shouldn't break
And I really hate to share you with the world
But when you come to me crying
And clinging on to me
I'm glad you are a big-hearted girl

Big-hearted girl, you know I understand
Remember me when you really want a man

There's a high price you'll pay
For giving yourself away
The gossip's gonna throw you for a whirl
But if the truth was known
They're wishing they were you
They'd like to be a big-hearted girl

Big-hearted girl, I won't tie you down
But let me know when you'll be back around

BODY ON BODY

1980s

You wonder how (where) true love goes
No one can say—cause nobody knows
Like rain on a rock—like a leaf in the air
No way to tell but it's going somewhere

You wonder what—true love knows
No one can say—cause nobody knows
It don't make sense—like a midnite sun
And one and one—is only one

Heart on heart—and soul on soul
Body on body is how it goes
Heart on heart and soul on soul
Body on body—is all it knows

CALIFORNIA POEM

1966

There's trouble on the mountain
And the valley's full of smoke
There's crying on the mountain
And again the same heart broke

The lights are on past midnite
The curtains closed all day
There's trouble on the mountain
The valley people say

the poor boy came from the farm land
She was the daughter of a sailor man
The Captain said when he beggs your hand
you better tell him no ho no no no

She said papa dont you worry please
The poor boy begs me upon his knees
But I'd never leave this life of ease
And with a poor boy go ho no no no

The Captain kissed her and he went to sea
The poor boy said go way with me
You're lonely and you shouldn't be
Oh dont you tell me no ho no no no

My daddy owns a clipper ship
He brings me pearls on every trip
And pink champagne for me to sip
And you're the poorest boy I know ho no

He said I've got no pearls for you
But I've got two arms and a heart thats
We could start with a dream or two
All wont you say you'll go ho no no no

THE CAPTAIN'S DAUGHTER

Undated (1950s/1960s)

The poor boy came from the farm land
She was the daughter of a sailor man
The Captain said, When he begs your hand
You better tell him no ho no no no

She said, Papa don't you worry, please
The poor boy begs me upon his knees
But I'd never leave this life of ease
And with a poor boy go ho no no no

The Captain kissed her and he went to sea
The poor boy said, Go away with me
You're lonely and you shouldn't be
Oh don't you tell me no ho no no no

My daddy owns a clipper ship
He brings me pearls on every trip
And pink champagne for me to sip
And you're the poorest boy I know ho ho ho ho

He said, I've got no pearls for you
But I've got two arms and a heart that's true
We could start with a dream or two
Oh won't you say you'll go ho no no no

You couldn't give me anything
Except a plain gold wedding ring
You've got no presents you could bring
My daddy's rich, you know ho ho ho ho

Your daddy's given you a home
But you've got nobody when he's gone
I'll go and leave you all alone
If the answer is still no ho no no no

My daddy's on the churning sea
And he would turn me across his knee
If he knew you were kissing me
I won't stay when you go ho no no no no

I'm a poor boy as you know
But I love the Captains daughter so
If I begged her would she go
Or would she tell me no no No No No

Daddy is a sailor man
You're fresh from the farm land
He said when you ask my hand
For me to tell you no no No No No.

Your daddys gone away to sea.
You're as lonely as can be
Come and go away with me.
Oh don't you tell me no no No No No

My daddy owns a Clipper ship
He brings me pearls on every trip
And pink champagne for me to sip
You're the poorest boy I know no No No No

I've got no pearls to give to you
I've got two arms and a heart thats true
We could start with a dream or two
Don't say you won't go no no no no

CHINKY PIN HILL

1970s

Come along with me and we
Will get away from it all
We'll go through the mountains past
The shining waterfall

The only sound we'll hear at night
Will be the whippoorwill
And the chirpin' of the crickets
On Chinky Pin Hill

We'll stop in Rainbow Valley
Where the church is standing still
And we'll be newlywed married
On Chinky Pin Hill

The world is so confusing as
I go from day to day
And sometimes I get worried
That I'll lose you on the way

I looked up at the stars
As I leaned on the windowsill
I've dreamed up a hideaway
Called Chinky Pin Hill

CROWLEY'S RIDGE

October 1967

I borrowed me a ridin' hoss
I headed north for Crowley's Ridge to cross
We crossed Little River at Le-Pan-To
Never slowed down
Till around Jones-boro
Destination: Hardy, Arkansas
To take my woman back
From her maw and paw

The rich Delta land
Was black and flat
But the cotton grows good
In ground like that

The sun set slowly
And the land turned red
On top of Crowley's Ridge
I unrolled my blanket
For my bed
I grazed my hoss

Near an elm tree
Then led him down to a spring
And let him drink after me
Short pine needles
Made a restful bed
And a sack of grass
Was the pillow for my head

I drank a can of coffee
Then rode on north
The gullies and thickets
Turned me back and forth
When I reached the north side
of Crowley's Ridge
The river had washed out
The WPA bridge

My hoss couldn't swim it
It was swift and deep
I hope the water's down by morning
So I hobbled him
And laid me down to sleep

The river was down next mornin' and the pilings was all
[that was] left of the WPA bridge.
I looked on the other side and there sat my woman and I waved

my arms at her. She jumped in the river and started swimmin'
toward me.
I met her halfway and swam back with her riding me. Then we
wrapped my blanket around us till we stopped shiverin' from
the cold water.
She said, I'm ready to go home with you now.
I said, You keep livin' with me and not run back to your folks?
She said, Yes, I belong with you, not in Hardy, Arkansas.

So we double-rode my borrowed hoss
Till the land got flat
For like the cotton
Love grows good
In ground like that

DARK AND BLOODY GROUND

1960s

I've been going like a quarry slave at night
All busted down and burning for my bed
I've been thinking about a woman
In a wild Kentucky town
Where the mountains are high near Harlan
And the whirlpools twirl on down
There my secret can be found
In the dark and bloody ground

Oh how I've missed you
Oh how I've cried
I'd like to lay you down by my side
And love you just once before I die
And I would be gentle and I would never hurt you
And God might send a moonbeam
And lay us down to pleasant dreams
Whatsoever things are lovely
Whatsoever things are true
Whatsoever things are kind and pure
Think you these things

And God might send a moonbeam
And lay us down to pleasant dreams

Dewey was my best friend he was tall
He stood six foot nine against the wall
We both loved the same girl
But Dewey he went bad
And I guess you could say he made one mad
He didn't have to do all those awful things to you
And Dewey made me sick
And I guess it takes two heels to click
I took my nine-pound hammer
Swung it hard and spun him round
Kicked him in the temple watched him falling
    to the ground
Then my blade found its mark in the dark
And that blood flowed in the sand from that
    tall Kentucky man
Hell hath no fury like the blues
When a man's got on his killing shoes
In the dark and bloody ground
Bloody ground bloody ground
In the dark and bloody ground

DOES ANYBODY OUT THERE LOVE ME?

1980s

It's a cold and cruel world
When there's no one to share the night
And it's a lonely road to travel
In the early-morning light

Somewhere there's somebody
And a place where you belong
So you give yourself a talking-to
And slowly move along

It's a long and endless journey
When you're on the lost pathway
Today will not be different
Than a hundred yesterdays

But maybe there's a new life
Dawning with the morning sun
And I'll be a better man
For where I've been and what I've done

Does anybody out there love me
Does anybody out there care
Does anybody out there want to share
Does anybody out there love me?

THE DOGS ARE IN THE WOODS

1970s

The dogs are in the woods
And the huntin's lookin' good
And the raccoons on the hill
I can hear them trailing still

Now he's on the other side
And he'll find a place to hide
But the dogs'll hunt him down
And they'll catch him on the ground

But the fur is gonna fly
And a hound is gonna cry
And we may not know tonight
Who will finally win the fight

But the dogs are in the woods
And the huntin' looks good

The fire is burning low
We wet it down and go
And we make a beeline
To the howling in the pine

It's too far to see
But they're barking up a tree
Then we hear them on the run
And the night has just begun

But the fur is gonna fly
And a hound is gonna cry
And we may not know tonight
Who will finally win the fight

But the dogs are in the woods
And the huntin' looks good

DON'T MAKE A MOVIE ABOUT ME

Christmas 1982

If anybody made a movie out of my life
I wouldn't like it, but I'd watch it twice
If they halfway tried to do it right
There'd be forty screenwriters workin' day and nite
They'd need a research team from Uncle Sam
And go from David Allan Coe to Billy Graham
It would run ten days in the final cut
And that would mean leaving out the gossip smut
And I do request for my children's sake
Don't ever let 'em do a new re-make
The thing I'm sayin' is, don't you see,
Don't make a movie 'bout me
Even for T.V.
Don't make a movie 'bout me

Don't let 'em drag old Hickory Lake
For my telephones and bottles and roller skates
Down forty feet in the Cumberland mud
There's a rusty old gun that once shed blood
Out a hundred yards from my lakeside house

Weighted down with a rock is a skirt and blouse
A dozen pair of boots that made a dozen corns
Trombones, trumpets, harmonicas and horns
And the tapes that I threw from the lakeside door
Silverstein, and Kristofferson from years before
Everything has a story that should be let be
So don't make a movie 'bout me

If they're hot on a book called *Man in Black*
Tell 'em I've got the rights and won't give back
If you don't know my tune you can't get it right
I don't talk about me in *Man in White*
Truth, said the Master, cannot be hid
But he didn't say slap it in the face of my kids.
A stone is a stone and forever stone
But I'm part good and bad and then I'm gone
There is no sin cleaner than the dirtiest
So there's a lot about me that I don't want missed
If it's days or years or whatever will be
Don't make a movie 'bout me

Aw, I might as well face it cause they will someday
So while I can I've got a thing to say
I don't know anybody that I said I don't know
And there ain't anybody anywhere I owe
The I.R.S. gets the lion's share
And what is left goes to my own named heirs

Don't let 'em make it in Hollywood
If they must, tell 'em Arkansas is where they should
Here's a hex on whoever makes it be,
So don't make a movie 'bout me
For Love or Monee
Don't make a movie 'bout me

DONT MAKE A MOVIE ABOUT ME
Christmas 1982   J.R. Cash

If anybody made a movie out of my life
I wouldn't like it, but I'd watch it twice
If they halfway tried to do it right
There'd be forty screen writers workin day & nite
They'd need a research team from uncle Sam
And go from David Allen Coe to Billy Graham
It would run ten days in the final cut
And that would mean leaving out the gossip smut
And I do request for my children's sake
Dont ever let 'em do a new re-make
The thing I'm sayin is, dont you see,
Dont make a movie 'bout me
              Even for T.V.
Dont make a movie 'bout me

Dont let 'em drag old Hickory Lake
For my telephones and bottles and roller skates
Down forty feet in the cumberland mud
There's a rusty old gun that once shed blood
Out a hundred yards from my lakeside house
Weighted down with a rock is a skirt
                                    a blouse
A dozen pair of boots that made a dozen corns
Trombones, trumpets, harmonicas and horns
And the tapes that I threw from the lakeside door
Silverstein, and Kristofferson from years before
Everything has a story that should be let be
So dont make a movie 'bout me

If they're hot on a book called Man in Black
Tell 'em I've got the rights and I wont give back
If you dont know my tune you cant get it right
I dont talk about me in Man in Man in white

Truth, said the master, cannot be hid
But he didn't say slap it in the face of my kids!
A stone is a stone and forever stone
But I'm part good and bad and then I'm gone

There is no sin cleaner than the dirtiest
So there's a lot about me that I dont want missed
If its days or years whatever will be
Dont make a movie 'bout me

Aw, I might as well face it cause they will some day
So while I can I've got a thing to say
I dont know anybody that I said I dont know
And there aint anybody anywhere I owe

The I.R.S. gets the lions share
And what is left goes to my own named heirs.
Dont let 'em make it in Hollywood
If they must, tell 'em Arkansas is where they should.
Here's a hex on whoever makes it be,
So dont make a movie 'bout me.
        for Love or Monee
Dont make a movie 'bout me

DON'T TAKE YOUR GUN TO TOWN

1980s

A young man of propriety
Found life to be a bore
He had studied politics and law
Psychology and more
He felt cold and jaded
Overall, and all around
On impulse, he picked up a gun
In the sleazy part of town
But a lady who understood him said,
Don't let the hammer down, Joe
Leave the thing at home, no—
Don't take the gun to town

They kissed and he said, Please
Don't underestimate your man
I can do and be and dare
As anybody can
Sweetheart, there are people
Who need silencing, and so,
I shall avenge society of hypocritical Joe, so,

Definitely I'll go, and
Take my gun to town

He named a politician
Who had long been on his list
A singer and an actor
And others I won't miss
The preachers with their promises
Are plastic bogus clowns
But a kind sweet voice kept haunting him,
Joe, don't take your gun to town
Do not draw the gun
Let God's peace rule the day, then
Throw the gun away, Joe
Let this obsession go

The happy cheering crowd unaware
Watched the motorcade move on
With a change of heart, Joe
Stood with his sweetheart alone
Then they walked to the river bridge
Where midway he sat down
He dropped the gun, and the water
Made a laughing sound
The cold blue steel for killing
Settled in the mud, deep down
And never will be found

Thank God for the woman
Who went out into the night
And quietly corrected
This great wrong and made it right . . .
With love she turned around
A tragedy unsound
And heaven answered down
Don't take your guns to town

Dont Take Your Gun to Town

A young man of propriety
found life to be a bore
He had studied politics and law
Psychology and more
He felt cold and jaded
Overall, and all aroud
On impulse he picked up a gun
In the sleazy part of town
But ~~the~~ a lady who understood him said
Dont let the hammer down Joe
Leave the thing at home / No—
Dont take the gun to town.

They kissed and he said please
Dont underestimate what man
I can do and be and dare
As anybody can
Sweetheart there are people
Who need silencing, and so,
I shall avenge ~~the~~ society of hypocrits/doc,
Definitely I'll go, and / so,
Take my gun to town—

He named a politician
Who had long been on his list
A singer and an actor
~~The girl But let me show you~~
And ~~Another~~ ~~the~~ I wont miss
The preachers with their promises
Are plastic bogus clowns
But a kind sweet voice kept haughty
Joe dont take your gun to town

Do not draw the gun
Let Gods peace rule the day, Then
Throw the gun away Joe!
~~Let~~ this obsession go

The happy cheering crowd ~~~~
Watched the motorcade, move on
With a change of heart, Joe
Stood with his sweetheart Iloac
Then they walked to the river bridge
Where ~~midway~~ he sat down
He dropped the gun ~~~~ and the water
Made a laughing sound
The cold blue steel for killing
Settled in the mud deep down
~~And never will be found~~
          mud –
    Thank God for the woman
Who went out into the night
And quickly corrected
    This great wrong and made it right
The intent ~~Went to the gun~~ of the gun
~~~~ With love she turned around
A tragedy unsound
And heaven answered down
Dont take your guns to Iowa

You tell me that I must Perish
Like the flowers that I cherish
Nothing remaining of my name
Nothing remembered of my fame
But the trees that I planted
~~Sta~~ still are young

The Songs I sang
Will still be sung

FOREVER

Summer 2003

You tell me that I must perish
Like the flowers that I cherish
Nothing remaining of my name
Nothing remembered of my fame
But the trees that I planted
Still are young
The songs I sang
Will still be sung

GOING, GOING, GONE

(version 2)

Loma Linda
Christmas 1990

Liquid, tablet, capsule, powder
Fumes and smoke and vapor
The payoff is the same in the end
Liquid, tablet, capsule, powder
Fumes and smoke and vapor
Convenient ways to get the poison in

Pop the pill and you don't hear
But there's a great explosion
Twenty thousand cells are dead and blind
Keep it up and very soon
A cold, dry wind is blowing
Down through the lifeless valleys of your mind

Take the tiny crystals now
Cause you don't need the stomach
Snort it, shoot it, ain't you having fun
Why can't the highs get higher

And why do the lows get lower?
Hey maybe you should get yourself a gun

It isn't fair you have to suffer
For a little pleasure
You must relax, the red capsule will do
So nice to sleep a little while
But you don't like this feeling
So you lay a line of powder, maybe two
You do your inventory
And some of your drugs are missing
You know you didn't do near half that much
Turn on the ones who love you
Why are they afraid and crying
And why do they recoil to your touch?

Lock your door, tie down the blinds
And bring the lights down lower
You're only happy now when you're alone
How many downers will it take?
Oh well, it doesn't matter
You've long been going, going; now you're gone

Going, Going, Gone

John R Cash

Liquid, tablet capsule powder
Smoke and fumes and vapor
The end is the end in the end
Liquid tablet capsule powder
Smoke and fumes and vapor
Convenient ways to get the poison in
Pop the pill and you dont hear but theres a great explosion
Twenty thousand cells are dead and blind
Keep it up and very soon a dry cold wind is crying
Down through the lifeless valleys of your mind
Take the tiny chrystals now dont worry about the strench
Snort it, shoot it. Aint you having fun.
Why cant the highs get higher and why do the lows get lower
And, oh yes, you were going to buy a gun.
It isnt fair that you should suffer for a little pleasure
You must relax, a double shot will do.
A moment of oblivion then you wake up pale and trembling
And you lay a line of powder, maybe two.
You do your enventory and some of your drugs are missing
You know you didn't do nearly half that much
You turn on those who love you. They are pleading and they're crying
And why do they recoil to your touch
You lock your door! You close the blinds
And bring the light down lower.
You're only happy now when you're alone
How many downers will it take? Oh well, it doesnt matter
You've been going going; now you're gone.

John R Cash
Loma Linda
Christmas 1990.

"Gold All Over the Ground"   J. Cash

March 1967

If I had you at my mercy
there's no tellin what I'd do
But I'd make you sit and listen
For an hour, maybe two

And then you'd know I need you
Every day that rolls around
Your feet would walk on velvet
With gold all over the ground

—— Your trails would be downhill
—— A soft breeze at your back
—— Your skies full of diamonds
—— Your nights would not be black

Yes you would really love it
Then if you're ever down
—— I'd give you rows of roses
And Gold all over the ground

I'd pick you up and carry you
'cross every stream I see
I'd bundle you in kindness
until you cling to me
We'd sit beneath strong branches
My arms would twine around
I'd turn your green to emerald — and give you

GOLD ALL OVER THE GROUND

March 1967

If I had you at my mercy
There's no tellin' what I'd do
But I'd make you sit and listen
For an hour, maybe two

And then you'd know I need you
Every day that rolls around
Your feet would walk on velvet
With gold all over the ground

Your trails would be downhill
A soft breeze at your back
Your skies full of diamonds
Your nights would not be black

Yes, you would really love it
Then if you're ever down
I'd give you rows of roses
And gold all over the ground

I'd pick you up and carry you
'Cross every stream I see
I'd bundle you in kindness
Until you cling to me

We'd sit beneath strong branches
My arms would twine around
I'd turn your green to emerald
And give you gold all over the ground

GOLD IN ALASKA

Early 1980s

Though it's cold in Alaska
There's gold in Alaska
There's nuggets in the rivers
And gold dust in the sand
I've got a girl in Seward
I ain't seen in quite a time
If she'll wait until October
When my diggin's done and over
I'll go cashin' in my stash
And we'll make love through the dark days
That winter sun don't shine
When I come back to the Tikchik
I'll leave her a little gold
Enough to keep her on the line

I went to Alaska
To a river called the Tikchik
In the middle of the summer
When the salmon make their run

And my guide with pick and shovel
Every day would stop and vanish
Then he'd come back with a handful of it
Shinin' in the sun

HE BORE IT ALL FOR ME

Come unto me, all ye that labour and are heavy
laden, and I will give you rest. —Matthew 11:28

Undated

He bore it all for me
He bore it all for me
When I was lost
A painful cross
He bore it all for me

He took the blame for me
He took the blame for me
He counted my wrongs
As forgotten and gone
He took the blame for me

He paid the price for me
He paid the price for me
A price that was high
For failure and lies
He paid the price for me

As he bore the pain for me
As he bore the pain for me
He spoke not a word
Not a cry was heard
He bore the pain for me

Yes, he bore it all for me
Yes, he bore it all for me
With nothing required
but faith in the Lord
Who bore it all for me

See Mat 11:28
for speaking intro

He Bore it all For Me

He Bore it All for me
" " " " "
When I was lost
On a painful cross.
He bore it all for me

He took the blame for me
" " " " " "
He counted my wrongs
As forgotten and gone
He took the blame for me

He paid the price for me
" " " " " "
A price that was high
For failure and lies
He paid the price for me

As He bore the pain for me
" " " " " "
He spoke not a word
Not a cry was heard
He bore the pain for me

Yes, He bore it all for
" " " " "
With nothing to save
But faith in He.
He bore it all for me

HEY, BABY, WAKE UP

Undated

Hey, Baby, wake up
If the sky should fall today
We could go outside and catch doves
And everything will be OK
Shake a leg and come on now
I need my biscuit buttered, Babe
Hey hey

Hey, Baby, wake up
I saw it on Channel 4
The president's out running
Back and forth and to and fro
Gonna make some big decisions
And he thought you'd need to know
Hey hey hey. Ho ho ho

Hey, Baby, wake up
Did you hear the latest news
The man said Roy and Dale split up

And Dale got Trigger, too
Yeah, I hear your sweet feet on the floor
I knew that'd get through to you
Hey hey. Ha ha ha

I HAVE BEEN AROUND

(version 2)

Undated

I have been around
I have been on the incoming
And the outward bound
I came up from the fields
And I've been down on my knees
I have been visited by angels
While demons badgered me
And I guess I gave the devil more than his due
But I always come back around to you

I have been around
I have kissed the moonlight
On a priceless pearl I found
I have been a counselor
And I have been a fool
I rode a wild horse
And I rode a Mach 2
I've been loved and I've been bored and I've been blue
But I always come back around to you

I have been around
I have tasted rapture that could not again be found
I felt the power filling up
And I felt the power gone
I've been full but hungry
And abandoned to the bone
In the end I knew one thing to pull me through
I always come back around to you

I HEARD ON THE NEWS

Early 1970s

I heard on the news
That there is a lull in the fighting
In Vietnam
Because so many Vietnamese
Are busy planting
A rice crop again
The report said
That full-scale fighting
Is expected to resume
Immediately after the planting season
I reply:
What kind of animal is man
That he would pause
In his killing
To go about the business
Of preparing for the living
Knowing
That he will immediately return
To the business of killing?

I WISH YOU A MERRY CHRISTMAS

Undated

I wish that you had choked on the glue
Of the goodbye letter you wrote
I wish that I had been standing by
To jam it down your throat
I send you best wishes too
For a long migraine headache
A hysterectomy on Christmas Eve
And a bathroom full of snakes

But I wish you a Merry Christmas
With your friends at Central State
I hope you'll be committed
On the dawn that Christmas breaks
You told me don't come back again
So I won't visit you
I wish you Merry Xmas in a straitjacket
It's been said you went to bed with one of my best friends
I hope he told you he's positive and the end will soon begin
Well I must close but you should know that yesterday when
    I left
I sold our House for Cash and kept the money for myself

But I wish you a Merry Christmas
And I'm sending you a gift
A nice neck brace and crutches, cause your old car
   won't shift
You'll know before you get this, that I fixed it up to break
I wanted you to know as you go
From the hospital to Central State
Yes I wish you a Merry Christmas
And a very short New Year

IF YOU LOVE ME

October 1983

The fluctuating worth
Of this very terminal earth
And the satellite that glows at night
Above me

Won't bear upon my mind
But concerning humankind
I won't care if you're there
And if you love me

A seed must die, I know
Before a plant can grow
And so would I
Before I'd let you go

Again the sun may rise
And burn thru yellow skies
But I'll see it through your blue eyes
If you love me

I see it in your eyes
If it's true or if it lies
I feel it if it's real
If you love me

Let the cold wind blow
Let seasons come and go
Let you come to my arms
If you love me

I'LL STILL LOVE YOU

Undated

One of these mornings
I'm gonna rise up flying
One of these mornings
I'll sail away beyond the blue
I've got a promise
That there's a better world ahead
I want you to know that when I go
I'll still love you

One of these mornings
When my trouble's over
One of these mornings
When all my suffering is through
I'll go out singing
It'll be a day to sing about
I guarantee for eternity
I'll still love you

I won't be a stranger
When I get to heaven

Cause you gave me heaven
Right here on earth
If I get rewarded
With a mansion on a golden street
I want you to know
For what it's worth
I'll still love you

I was driving in the rain
Twenty miles from Bangor Maine
When I realized how much you mean to me
So I turned the rig around
Filled her up outside of town
Took the shortest route southbound to Tenn
I'm Comin' Honey
Hang out the front door keep
I'm Comin' Honey
Get ready to pucker up for me

I was drivin' in the sleet
Stopped to get a bite to eat
Folks in Penn asked me if I'd stay
I said thank you anyhow
But I think I'll make it now
I can't stay away from her another day
I'm Comin' honey
Turn on the front light for me
I'm Comin' honey
Look out the window and see

I was drivin' in the snow
On a mountain called Soco
your picture hanging on my rear
view q last
I was heavy on the foot —
I was blowing out the soot
There was no one alive who'd try
to pass

I'm comin' honey
Put a little coffee on the pot
I'm comin' honey
Get set to give me all the lovin'

I'M COMIN', HONEY

Late 1950s

I was driving in the rain
Twenty miles from Bangor, Maine
When I realized how much you mean to me
So I turned the rig around
Filled her up outside of town
Took the shortest route southbound to Tennessee
I'm comin', Honey
Hang out the front door key
I'm comin', Honey
Get ready to pucker up for me

I was drivin' in the sleet
Stopped to get a bite to eat
Folks in Penn asked me if I'd stay
I said, Thank you, anyhow
But I think I'll make it now
I can't stay away from her another day
I'm comin', Honey
Look out the window and see

I'm comin', Honey
Turn on the front light for me

I was drivin' in the snow
On a mountain called Soco
Your picture hanging on my rearview glass
I was heavy on the foot
I was blowing out the soot
There was no one alive who'd try to pass
I'm comin', Honey
Put a little coffee in the pot
I'm comin', Honey
Get set to give me all the love you got

JELLICO COAL MAN

Undated

I've got a little black ring around my neck
And I will sell you coal by the bushel or the peck
I will sell you coal by the gallon or the pound
And you don't have to look for me, I'll be around

Yellin', Jellico coal man
Jellico coal man
I'm the Jellico coal man
Coal, coal, coal

There is coal that's soft and coal that's hard
I will bring it around through your backyard
I love chocolate cake and apple pie
I believe I will have a piece when I come back by

I'm the Jellico coal man
Jellico coal man
Jellico coal man
Coal, coal, coal

It will warm your baby in the winter time
It comes direct from the Jellico mine
When the sun comes up that's the time I start
You will see me comin' with my two-wheel cart

Yellin', Jellico coal man
Jellico coal man
Jellico coal man
Coal, coal, coal

JOB

Early 1990s

Job was a wealthy man
He had a lot of kids and a lot of land
He had cattle on a thousand hills
He lived every day to do God's will
Satan came with the sons of men
The Lord said Satan where you been?
He said I have been around
And to and fro and up and down
Working hard for all I'm worth
To rule all men upon this earth
The Lord said do the worst you can
But my servant Job is a faithful man
Satan did the worst he could
Job kept right on being good
But he cried out in agony
When he lost his children and his property
Satan started laughing and he said again
It's bone for bone and skin for skin
Then he looked up to the holy place
Said I make him curse you to your face

Satan struck Job from his feet to his head
With corruption, and Job got out of bed
And sat right down in the marketplace
With sackcloth and ashes on his face
The Lord said you can't take his life
Satan said I'll work on his wife
Job's wife said curse God and die
He's not going to hear you cry

Job Job watch what you say
The Lord let Satan have his way
Don't give in and don't give up
The Lord could soon refill your cup
Then the best three friends that Job ever had
Zophar, Eliphaz and Bildad
Sat down with him for seven days
To share his grief without a word to say
Job said why does it have to be
That the thing I feared has come on me
He cried out I deplore my birth
Let my birthday perish from the earth
His friends said Job you should repent
The perfect don't get punishment
Job said I harmed no man
There's been no violence by my hand
As surely as sparks upward fly
I was born to trouble and I want to die

I want to see God face-to-face
And stand right up and argue my case
There is no justice I can see
God has been unfair to me
I've been righteous, I've been good
And God won't talk to me like he should

Job Job your friends are nice
But they gave you some bad advice
What's needed here, it seems to me
Is a little thing called humility
Then along came a friend named Elihu
Said I will speak to God for you
And he will bring you from the pit
He'll raise you up from where you sit
He will chasten, test, and try
But by his grace you didn't die
He purifies you in your pain
And he can make you whole again
Then God said who can this be
Who challenges my majesty
Who speaks but does not know what to say
Where were you on creation day
Learn a lesson from the animals and birds
Don't darken my counsel with empty words
Show me your wisdom if you can
And gird yourself up like a man

Job looked up into the firmament
And said Lord God I do repent
I bow down before your throne
My will is yours and yours alone
The bounty flowed from heaven's door
And Job was twice as wealthy as before
He had a golden chain and a long white robe
And the happiest man in the world was Job

Job Job watch what you say
The Lord let Satan have his way
Don't give in and don't give up
The Lord could soon refill your cup
You could make a comeback still
with cattle on a thousand hills

LET'S PUT IT TO MUSIC

1960s

How do you feel about me
Now that you've learned to know me?
Why don't we both admit
That something is happening
And we would feel better if
We'd just tell each other
No need to keep it to ourselves
Let's put it to music
Let's put it to music
Let's sing about it
Laugh about it
Clap our hands
And shout about it
Let the whole world hear it
In a sweet, sweet melody
Let's put it to music, you and me

LOST MY MONEY IN A BUFFALO TRACK

1970s

I lost my money in a buffalo track
On the Blue Ridge Mountain
Where the road turns back
From Philadelphy to the Cumberland Gap
There ain't a maple standin'
That'll give me sap
The rim ran off of a wheel one night
But I keep it watered
It'll be alright
We crossed Clinch River where
The skeeters scratch
Then we smoked 'em out
In a baccer patch
The cornmeal's weevily
And the bacon's rank
But the perch was tasty
on Cumberland banks

At a place called French Lick, Tennessee
We fought the weather and the Cherokee
We fed on deer and buffalo
And we tanned their hide
Against the winter snow

MUSCADINE WINE

2000s

Right by the porch
In the honeysuckle vines
I found a jug
Of Muscadine wine
So I pulled the plug
And I took a little whiff
And said I can't handle
This by myself

Before you could say
Zippety-doo
All my neighbors smelled it, too
In comes Casey and Carey
And Joe
With a how-de-do
And a high-de-ho

Ain't you heard
Long as you live
It's whole lot more

Blessed to give
And we all feel blessed
And mighty fine
Passing around
Muscadine wine

Right by the porch
In the honeysuckle vines
I found a jug
Of muscadine wine.
So I pulled the plug
And I took a little whiff
And said I can't handle
this by my self.
Before you could say
Zippety-doo
All my neighbours smelled it
In comes Casey & Carey too
and Joe
With a how-de-do.
And a high-de-ho

Aint you heard
Long as you live
It's a whole lot more
blessed to give.
And we all feel blessed
And mighty fine
Passing Around
Muscadine Wine

MY SONG

1970s

Well, it's many a day
The road gets weary
And it's many a day
That the way is long
And I often say,
No more I do it
But I miss the traveling
And I miss the songs

I was born to sing
But not to the wind and space
But to people's hearts
And people's ears
'Tis a gift from God
And I pray I'd use it
And sing to their hearts
And sing to their ears

For a song can soar
Like the lofty eagle

And lift a heart
That has fallen low
And a song can shine
Like a light in darkness
And make the downcast
Look up and glow

I wish I owned
A great high mountain
With people below
Every way I turned
I wish they'd look up
And ears could hear me
And I'd sing my song
To the hearts that yearned

I would sing it loud
I would sing it long
Straight from the heart
I would sing it true
Then I'd come back down
From my singing mountains
And your life would be better
Cause I sang for you

ROOM 1702

Late 1960s

In the hotel room alone I was lying
In the night a man was softly crying
He grabbed his phone
And then he started screaming
I covered up my head and said,
I'm dreaming

The man said, Send someone
I know I'm dying
Come to 1702,
The man was crying

In the darkness I reached for the light
But my hand couldn't penetrate the night
I left my bed, but didn't feel the floor
Then someone was knocking at my door
Thru the bolted door I stepped right thru
And we walked out of 1702

SILK AND DENIM

1990s

She wore silk and denim
She wore silk and denim
From the top of her red head
To her red-painted toes
The way she turned when I called her name
Her skirt whirled in circles
There were lacy little roses
On her red pantyhose

She looked like a fire coming
All except her eyes
They were bluer than lazuli
And deeper than the skies
They were full of love and welcome
They were kind and they were smiling
And I knew in a heartbeat
I would love her till I die

She wore lace and denim
She wore lace and denim

Lacy decorated bosom
Soft blue denim on her hips
I tried not to undress her
But my mind could not be passive
I fantasized my loving her
I kissed her on the lips

And the denim buttons opened
And the blue cloth fell away
She turned her back and held her hair up
Smiled a sweet OK
I fumbled with the lace buttons
And not one word did we say

SLUMGULLION

1970s

Get a chicken if you can catch it
Get a pot if you can steal it
Take that bottle from your pocket
Let me hold it till I can't feel it
Let me lay down by the fire
Let me get a little higher
Till my head turns to slumgullion

Four a.m. I'm sleeping peaceful
Dreaming of that girl in Billings
And she's kissing me and crying
And she's warm and she is willing
Then the cold rain and the wind
Brings me reality again
Turns my dreams into slumgullion

Never laugh at the devil
Cause he ain't to be outsmarted
Bout the time you think you whipped him
You will find that he's just started

He will run you off the sidin'
Jump right up from where he's hidin'
Turn your plans into slumgullion

When you think you are a winner
And a number one all over
Don't go smilin' in the mirror
Don't go rollin' in the clover
Every day's a brand-new mountain
Don't drink long at any fountain
You'll be turned into slumgullion

SLUMGULLION

Get a chicken if you can catch it
Get a pot if you can steal it
Take that bottle from your pocket
Let me hold it till I cant feel it
Let me lay down by the fire
Let me get a little higher
Till my head turns to Slumgullion

Four AM I'm sleeping peaceful
Dreaming of that girl in Billings
And she's kissing me and crying
And she's warm and she is willing
Then the cold rain and the wind
Brings me reality again
Turns my dreams into Slumgullion

Never laugh at the devil
Cause he aint to be outsmarted
Bout the time you think you whipped him
You will find that he's just started
He will run you off the sidin
Jump right up from where he's hidin
Turn your plans into Slumgullion

When you think you are a winner
And A number one all over
Dont go smilin in the mirror
Dont go rollin in the clover
Every days a brand new mountain
Dont drink long at any fountain
You'll be turned into Slumgullion

SPIRIT RIDER

Before you know if you will see a ~~mystic horseman~~ Spirit Rider
Cut me off, babe, and I'll be gone
I will mount my Hi-Yo and I will ride off ma'am
And I'll go on (and on and on) and on and on
The ~~voice~~ you made in one ear ~~will~~ blow out the other
Let a storm rage ~~round~~ me on my outward track
~~When~~ I hear bluebirds I wont go any farther
And ~~when~~ the sky gets clear back here
I'll be ridin back

I will ramble, drift and range and you'll be walkin
Around imaginary things up on the floor
Walkin circles round the reasons that have vanished
You'll forget what doesn't matter anymore
you might ~~then you'll~~ get a glimpse of me off in the distance
If you cry out I ~~just~~ might hear you on the wind
And if the mountains echo your love to me
Wave your heart and,
I'll be ridin back again

On a moonbeam there might come a spirit rider
Who'll be watching for a flickering in the gloom
He will put a feeler out for love and welcome
And he just might cast a shadow 'cross your room
I will scent out any evidence of danger
I will taste the air around any sugar shack
~~If~~ my heart knows ~~that~~ you wont treat it like a stranger
And ~~if~~ the fire is lit
I'll be ridin back.

SPIRIT RIDER

1980s

On a moonbeam there might come a spirit rider
Who'll be watching for a flickering in the gloom
He will put a feeler out for love and welcome
And he just might cast a shadow 'cross your room
I will scent out any evidence of danger
I will taste the air around my sugar shack
If my heart knows you won't treat it like a stranger
And if the fire is lit
I'll be ridin' back

Before you know it you will see a spirit rider
Cut me off, babe, and I'll be gone
I will mount my Hi-Yo and I will ride off, ma'am
And I'll go on (and on and on) and on and on
The lies you laid in one ear will blow out the other
Let a storm rage round me on my outward tack
If I hear bluebirds I won't go any farther
And if the sky gets clear back here
I'll be ridin' back

I will ramble, drift and range and you'll be walkin'
Around imaginary things upon the floor
Walkin' circles round the reasons that have vanished
You'll forget what doesn't matter anymore
You might get a glimpse of me off in the distance
If you cry out I might hear you on the wind
And if the mountains echo your love to me
Wave your heart and
I'll be ridin' back again

TECUMSEH

Undated

A baby Indian boy was born one morning
In the early-morning dark when no birds fly
Born to be a prophet like his brother
And they saw the eye of a panther in the sky
A comet with a fierce head came screaming
Round and fierce and with a tail of light
The day that dawned was known as the day of the panther
With the birthday of a baby boy in the morning light

Tecumseh go and shout it from the mountains
White men are coming from the salty sea
They'll take your hand and steal all your tomorrows
All must stand together to be free

Already there are nations gone forever
Your people are signing treaties that are lies
Listen to the one great Holy Spirit
Then go to every tribe and prophecy
And the Great Spirit said, On a hilltop near the father
    of the waters

I'll stamp my foot and strike all hearts with fear
At the settlement the white man calls New Madrid
You will see it, you will feel it, you will hear

Tecumseh mounted up and for twelve moons
Went forth and pleased, preached and prophesied
He told them that a great earthquake was coming
But it wouldn't be a day for them to hide
He said it will be a sign to meet me
In Indiana where we'll make our stand
The Great Spirit said for me to tell you
This we must do if we're to keep our land

Tecumseh go and shout it from the mountains
White men are coming from the salty sea
They'll take your hand and steal all your tomorrows
All must stand together to be free

The earthquake came in the year 1811
Just as Tecumseh prophesied
He stood upon the banks east of the river
And watched as buildings fell and people died
He saw the Mississippi running backwards
Whirling, muddy death was in the flow
Then he rode the trembling ground fast and northward
Where he prayed every Indian would go

But from all the tribes that came from east of the river
Just a remnant came to Indian land
And they met the war machines in a terrible battle
And they fought and fell in fighting hand to hand
Then the white men pushed them north and westward
And they safely came to the land of the Cree
Tecumseh fell at his last stand in Canada
And his people still speak of his prophecy

The spirit of Tecumseh is still pleading
In all directions as the eagle flies
His mother knew that he was very special
The night she saw the panther in the sky

TENDERFOOT FROM THE CITY

1940s

I don't want to be a gun-totin' Texan
Rather see 'em in the moving picture show
And I don't want to be a singin' cowboy
Rather hear the popular songs on the radio

Want a soft, fluffy place to lay my head
Don't want any snakes or cactus beds
Rather ride my girl in my Cadillac
Than to ride a smelly horse's back

No I won't get tanned from riding a mule
I'll get my tan in a swimming pool
I'm a tenderfoot from the city
But I'm livin' just the same

I'm a tenderfoot from the city
And I live a life of ease
I wear my silk and satin
And go just where I please

THE THINGS WERE
FRIGHTENED AT

WHEN I WAS JUST A LITTLE KID
AND PLAYED A LOT AT NIGHT
BACK IN OUR COUNTRY VILLAGE
WHERE WE DIDN'T PAY FOR LIGHT
THEN I COULD SEE BEHIND EACH TREE,
AN INDIAN STANDING THERE
AND SAY, HOW I'D SHAKE AND HOLLER!
IT WOULD FAIRLY RAISE MY HAIR
AND WHEN I GREW TO BE A MAN
    I KNEW IT MORE AND MORE
THAT HALF THE FUN WAS KNOWING NOT
    WHAT I WAS RUNNING FOR
AND I USED TO GO TO TOWN
    EVERY NIGHT FOR PAW
I'D GO DOWN THE ROAD JUST, LICKEDY SPLIT!
    UNTIL MY FEET WERE RAW
I HAD A LITTLE COUSIN
    (HE WAS SCARY, TOO)
HE'S WORSE THAN I AM
    HE'S SCARED OF GHOSTS   ARE YOU
ONCE I HEARD MY COUSIN JUST OUTSIDE
    A YELLIN'
HE WOULDN'T TELL ME WHAT IT WAS
    I SAID THERE AINT NO TELLING

THE THINGS WE'RE FRIGHTENED AT

April 26, 1944

When I was just a little kid
And played a lot at night
Back in our country village
Where we didn't pay for light
Then I could see behind each tree
An Indian standing there
And say, how I'd shake and holler!
It would fairly raise my hair
And when I grew to be a man
I knew it more and more
That half the fun was knowing not
What I was running for
And I used to go to town
Every night for Paw
I'd go down the road just lickety-split!
Until my feet were raw
I had a little cousin
(He was scary, too)
He's worse than I am
He's scared of ghosts. Are you?

Once I heard my cousin
Just outside a-yellin'
He wouldn't tell me what it was
I said there ain't no telling

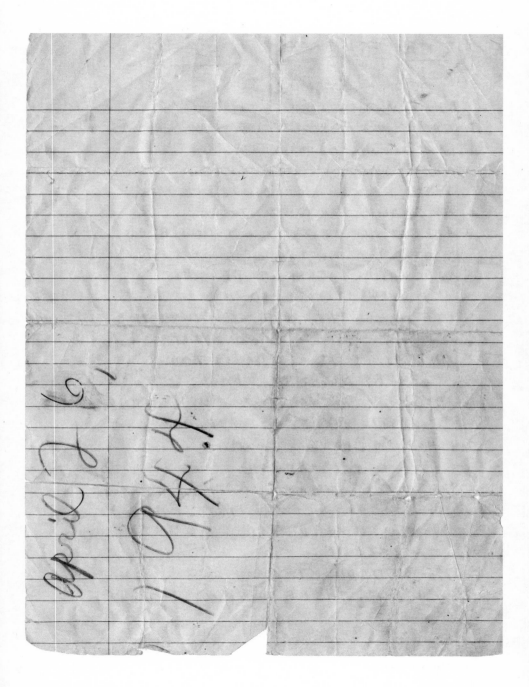

April 26

THE WALKING WOUNDED

1970s

We're in the church-house kneeling down
We're in the subways underground
We're in the bars and on the street
We drive a truck, we walk a beat
We're in the mills and factories
We make the steel, we cut the trees
A thousand-yard stare, eyes of glass
We will see you when we pass
We are the walking wounded

We lost our homes, we lost our dreams
All our goals turned into schemes
We hurt each other and ourselves
We went through long, traumatic spells
We cried out from the deepest pit
But rise back up each time we're hit
We fell from power and from grace
But resurrection's in our face
We are the walking wounded

Just like little girls and boys
We played with our grown-up toys
We never thought of sink or swim
I traded her, she went with him
Like a circle round and round
Just going up and coming down
No shame and no integrity
I hurt her and she left me
We are the walking wounded

We don't explain or apologize
We pull the veil across our eyes
We see through your fake and rain
But we won't let you see our pain
We don't ask you to forgive
We demand that you let live
You can't understand, and so,
You don't really need to know
We are the walking wounded

Together, we are legion
We are honest with each other
Though we stay and though we leave
You may see us and not know us
There are many more of us than you'd believe

WHAT WOULD I DREAMER DO

Undated

What would I dreamer do
The rainbow already has its hue
The sea has long been salted down
And there are far too many clowns
For too many carnivals

Some tell me, Be like me
No one should be like you, you see
Hide your mysterious secret side
While hungry fools have died
Unlocking mysteries

I put on a nice, neat suit
Hide my straw hat and boots
Live the accepted normal life
Answer to Mr., how's your wife?
and your children?

Seems to me to fix up things
I should fly on brazen wings

Passing by all that conforms
Wear no raincoat in storms
And to hell with umbrellas

Why should I wait in my seat
Passing time for a glutton to eat
I may know no other task
But I won't wait, so don't ask
I'll go do something

I don't recall, if any or what
Task or duty fell my lot
They say songs are for nothing but to sing
Say the never listening—unhearing
While the music plays

I don't have it all figured, I guess
Maybe I'm confused as the rest
But I won't live 8 to 5
Are the 8 to 5 alive
Even on weekends?

So, I'll walk a lot of streets
Get up and go, whenever I eat
Throw away that business suit
Put neat's-foot oil on my boots
And track mud on somebody's carpet

WHO'S GONNA GREASE MY SKILLET?

Undated

Who's gonna grease my skillet
When you're gone
Who's gonna grease my skillet
When you're gone
Who's gonna turn the heat on
When I'm cold to the bone
Who's gonna grease my skillet
When you're gone?

Who's gonna squeeze my juice
If you should go
Who's gonna squeeze my juice
If you should go
What you gonna do about it
If it drops down too low
Who's gonna squeeze my oranges
When you go?

Who's gonna wipe your juices
From my shirt

Who's gonna wipe your juices
From my shirt?
Don't let anybody touch you
It'll dry up in the dirt
Don't let anybody touch you
It'll dry up in the dirt

Who's gonna grease my skillet
When you're gone
Who's gonna grease my skillet
When you're gone
Who's gonna turn the heat on
When I'm cold to the bone
Who's gonna grease my skillet
When you're gone?

YOU NEVER KNEW MY MIND

1967

I know you feel the way I change
But you can't change the way I feel
Sometimes I'm a stranger to you—one of a kind
I think some way you'll make it
Though you don't know how to take it
You can't deal with how I'm thinkin'
Cause you never knew my mind

There were times of lots of laughter
And you felt you understood me
We were carefree, open, honest
Loving easy, true and kind
I suppose you never doubted then
That we had it all together
Then you say the changes painfully, and knew
You never knew my mind

My silence holds the secrets when I answer,
    but don't answer

You didn't see me well enough to recognize the signs
You didn't want to know it's over
You never looked close enough to know
You never knew my mind

ACKNOWLEDGMENTS

Thanks to Mark Stielper—researcher and Cash historian. Mark was invaluable to the process of making this book a reality. Also to Tom Benck, Jason Preston, and Marty Stuart. Johnny gave the handwritten "Don't Make a Movie About Me" to Marty years ago, and he was nice enough to allow us access to the original writing/sketch. Thanks to Monique van Dorp, Alison McCoury, and Lauren Moore for added research and dedication to helping with the organization of works. You were invaluable to this process. Ana Cristina Alvarez—soon to be Mrs. John Carter Cash. Thanks for having faith. And to Lou Robin, Karen Robin, Sarah Hochman, David Rosenthal, Sony Legacy, Trey Call, Devik Wiener, David Ferguson, Nadine King, AnnaBelle Cash, Jack Cash, Joseph Cash, Chuck Turner, Bono, Doug Caldwell, T Bone Burnett, Callie Khouri, Cathy Sullivan, Josh Matas, and all at Sandbox Entertainment. Likewise, to Lisa Trice, Tiffany Dunn, Brittany Schaeffer, and everyone at Loeb & Loeb—thank you.

John Carter Cash